100 MILES OF HEAT

poetry by

Mark B. Hamilton

Finishing Line Press
Georgetown, Kentucky

POETRY BY MARK B. HAMILTON

100 Miles of Heat
Confronting the Basilisk
Earth Songs

Copyright © 2017 by Mark B. Hamilton
ISBN 978-1-63534-148-5 First Edition
All rights reserved under International and Pan-American Copyright Conventions.
No part of this book may be reproduced in any manner whatsoever without written permission from the publisher, except in the case of brief quotations embodied in critical articles and reviews.

ACKNOWLEDGMENTS

My thanks to the editors of:

Canvas: "An excerpt from 'Fortunate Creek.'"
The Listening Eye: "Hands that Row" and "A Serious Business."
New Letters: "The River as Teacher," finalist in creative nonfiction.
Poetry Salzburg Review: "A Little River Town" and "Horses Crossing the River."
Ship of Fools: "An Island in History," "Dreams of Point Pleasant" and "100 Miles of Heat."
We Proceeded On: "An Oral History of the Mammoth in North America."
Written River: "Of Bayous and Pine Sand."

Publisher: Leah Maines

Editor: Christen Kincaid

Cover Art: Sandie Seeger

Author Photo: Sandie Seeger

Cover Design: Elizabeth Maines McCleavy

Printed in the USA on acid-free paper.
Order online: www.finishinglinepress.com
also available on amazon.com

Author inquiries and mail orders:
Finishing Line Press
P. O. Box 1626
Georgetown, Kentucky 40324
U. S. A.

CONTENTS

A Little River Town	1
Hands that Row	3
Ohio's First City	4
An Island in History	5
A Song	7
Horses Crossing the River	8
Dreams of Point Pleasant	10
A Serious Business	12
Fortunate Creek	14
The Estuarial Brain	16
Of Bayous and Pine Sand	18
The River as Teacher	21
An Oral History of the Mammoth…	23
100 Miles of Heat	25
About the Author	31

—for Sandie

A LITTLE RIVER TOWN

> Oh *not* because happiness *exists*,
> that too-hasty profit snatched from approaching loss.
> Not out of curiosity, not as practice for the heart, which
> would exist in the laurel too. . . . .
>
> But because *truly* being here is so much; because everything here
> apparently needs us, this fleeting world, which in some small way
> keeps calling to us. Us, the most fleeting of all.
> —Rainer Maria Rilke, *The Ninth Elegy*

When ashore, nothing is better than a new map,
clean clothes, and eating fruit beneath a pavilion in the rain.
To retain joy becomes my discipline. It sets me prowling
the streets to favored shops for little things I need or want:
hamburger, pastry, chocolate bar. Showers follow me around:
picket fence, sidewalk, shade tree, urging me down the street.

In the morning, on flat water I sweep out onto the floodplain.
Bass boats skim past, hulls balanced on their props, ripping
growls from the water. The wind dies, the sky darkens into slate.
Raindrops approach in a busy hum.

Then they close-in like a freight train rattling and boiling,
shrinking the horizon into a mere gap of low cloud, a waterfall
I enter, exhilarated, inside a tin can beneath a heel of thunder,
flat down, expecting nothing while lightning flashes left
and right. I feel the boldness of river rumbling.

Raindrops pop the surface into craters and leaping fragments.
I lean forward, compressed under the heavy paws, the dory
cutting through vertical water.

And suddenly, it all stops,
the storm subsides, its identity of an hour just the refreshing
cool water swashing around my ankles—a cycle of weather
melding the greens and silvers in a loom of trees,

framing a red-headed buzzard brooding in the black branches
hunching his shoulders, the air so clear each feather
seems edged by a single thread.

I row out into the river, cross the oars to bailout the boat.
It's so quiet even the barge traffic seems less threatening,
so I row farther out into the channel feeling safer, saving
many strokes as I lean into the oars.

The current remains slight, but I want what there is of it,
leaving more daylight for extra miles or walks on shore.
Anchored for the night, the creek wears origins of weather
far to the east, clouds that linger above drifting fishermen.

HANDS THAT ROW

All things on a map are not true. Buoys drift out of place,
marinas are built, factories demolished, islands washed away.

The one sure thing when rowing
is that everything comes down to the hands:
calluses that burn, fingers that curl to accumulate power.

I plot my daily motion as a linear scratch of time,
an empirical surface etched into the charted unknowns.

A beautiful doe stares, huge ears listening to the white hull.
She browses, nips a few leaves, and ambles out of sight,
invisible in that single step beyond the pine boughs.

She knows the river creates through time, not as time,
not by the measure of a clock turning to fatigue at day's end.
From her response, my struggles seem too unnatural.
I think I have much work to do.

At Willow Island Dam the lockmaster says,
"Haven't seen a rowboat on this river for twenty-five years!
Where're ya' from?"
"Pittsburgh."
"Where're ya' going?"
"Cairo."
"Kayro! That's a ways. Good luck to ya'!"

I return to my body and breathe the river.
Fresh paint merges with the countryside, towns and farms
waken with rural life, with staying put and working hard,
family and friends holding the mud down.

OHIO'S FIRST CITY

Marietta sits on knolls above the Muskingum
where I nestle into a transit slip at the City Marina,
my hands wrapped and blistered, especially the left
which is vengeful.

In a rag cap and baggy breaches, I'm a river roustabout
walking in a city of cars and glass shops, pleased
with the company I keep in the vast amusement park.

Towboats pass like reclining statues, tired eyes closing
above a quarter mile of heaped coal, or an island of scrap iron.

A fisherwoman casts a lure into the mysteries, into the shadows
of a moored sternwheeler, the showboat Becky Thatcher.

She weaves a question and retrieves the chance,
breathing above the sighs of the Muskingum.

Marietta watches, close to sleep,
resting upon the ancient geometry of the Adena.

AN ISLAND IN HISTORY

i.

The channel line sways from riverbank
to riverbank as I maneuver in the wakes of towboats
looking always to escape, to jump out of the dory
onto shore immersed as I am in this commerce of Lime,
Metal, Oil, and Aggregates.

I practice aggression, the boldness of a red tailed hawk
diving out of the heated sky into a clutch of ducks
scooting around in the shallows.

The current drags me through the narrows at Neal Island.
In two hours ten miles pass amid the kingfishers and towboats
thumping toward Parkersburg Bend and Little Kanawha River.

For Lewis, squirrels kept migrating across the Ohio,
sunsets were dimmed by the great flocks of passenger pigeons.
His crewmen arrived late that morning. Rounded up bodily,
they were too drunk to depart. Malaria was endemic,
the U.S. Postal Service was a man billeted in a clapboard house
where Lewis ate dinner behind window panes in the candlelight.

ii.

Blennerhassetts Island has lost its fine gardens, scattered now
with black walnut trees, the mansion burned down by slaves.
Harman and Margaret were Aaron Burr supporters, had plotted
for new territories in the west with that sly General Wilkinson.
And it is said, she gallops her horse along the river at night,
her red ballroom gown flowing like fire.

iii.

I walk westward behind my heart through the hayfields,
up into the meadows of sunshine, thinking of them
and of history in the dust of a dirt road to a log cabin
where kids are playing with their pet raccoon.

I sit beneath cool cottonwoods and eat, and then launch
from a beach to head downriver again, well off the channel
with my feet up as I drift and snooze in the heat, sheltered
by the wide brim of my 3-dollar straw hat.

A SONG

Today I've left the city,
its jowly air and its brittle air
in the murk of shouldering streets.

I've cast away most of the weight
carried in my pockets, and like a tarp
I slide beneath, I'm freed.

The Ohio wind is a soothing wind.
I row to my heart's content,
a maple clutches the muddy bank
holding messages I've sent.

Today I've left the city
and row to my heart's content.
I think I need to know that voice
of what the river meant.

HORSES CROSSING THE RIVER

Rocky banks edge into shadow, into outcroppings,
sharp textures unaccustomed to the summer's soft greens.
They form hazardous herds of wild mustangs chiseled
from the stream, looming up in the shallows, pointed ears
like saw teeth in the quick current around bends, escaping
always escaping as one goes up onto the shore after the next.

Near Shade River, I attempt a landing at a smooth black beach
beyond a rocky point. With the first step I'm in deep mud,
quicksand up to my thighs, a hand on Pelican lifting me free.

Under the heat, the "to and from" seem all the same,
an island towhead packed hard with sand, piled with drift
from floodwaters, flotsam and even logs that are hung,
scattered and stuffed into the crotches of trees, debris
30 feet up is the sensible ruin from lots of spring water.

At Sandy Creek I snub Pelican to a tree in a gentle place,
clean without litter where browns and greens flicker golden
opaque light, and the white boat stays solid and sharply lined,
low to the water and buoyant.

Nestled so closely, the solitude rises. It is wonderfully still
with surrounding silhouettes, the maples' dark reflections
and the sky turning from blue to indigo.

Through Pelican's hull I hear a gurgling and bubbling,
and then low voices, three teenagers drift-fishing,
their outboard barely audible at idle.

It is nightfall on the slow flow. Muskrats are out. They belly down the bank, cruise by and browse on tender vegetable things, thinking me a pretty fancy log. And there are lots of water bugs, while not many mosquitoes, here, where I could live close to the river, in a little cabin on stilts, all year long.

It's amazing how far we will travel
to understand just one old saying.

DREAMS OF POINT PLEASANT

I wrap bandanas around my hands as new blisters spring up
between old ones, which I nurse with iodine, cauterized pins
and gauze. I row with my left hand tingling and asleep
as it cramps and disengages, the palm no longer useful,
only the last few digits of each finger functional. By day's end
my extremities are numb.

Yet the big world goes well here, although a nice breeze
would be welcomed as more than a mere thought in the trees,
or as the low dust of a farmer haying, or as the silence
of a heron stalking its own startled image.

In the fatigue and disorientation of late afternoon,
four teenage girls splash in the shallows
like water nymphs. They release me from my efforts
as I drift past the scene, just another bird of reflection.

Our pace slows, and I'm tired. Heavy rain and thunder find me
in open water as I row fast beneath its waterfall, under my hat,
light jeans and long sleeved T-shirt toward a creek with a bridge
as refuge, barely wide enough for the oars. Rust colored run-off
forms the wall of this haven where I anchor close-in to rip-rap,
securing the dory between sunken re-iron and a grappling hook.

Possible flooding would change the safe nature of this place.

In the morning, oar strokes are in higher water.
Reflections rush forward into a rhythmic splash and sweep,
colors enlivening in the ripple of the wake.

Often the curve and turn of Creek or Run will set us deeply
down into the landscape, close to steep banks on either side,
close to the hush of bird song and the whoosh of oar
into a quietude that becomes the mystery, old myths
submerged like fallen trees.

We pass West Virginia power plants. Some one-mile long, studded with iron cylinders 10 feet in diameter, 25 feet high, so coal can be off-loaded all year. The brooding hum of turbines rises ominous and linear, the implacable jaws of a bucket drops from a crane into a barge, lifting the transformations of the sun.

Moving like hunger, I mimic necessity, rowing past the barges fleeted and moored stem to stern, doubled out along the bank as I turn into Crooked Creek and row toward Point Pleasant, and all my fantasies.

The creek tangles into ponds, a labyrinth of clinging branches and painted turtles. A roughly hewn sign nailed to a tree states, "City Marina," near a muddy ramp cluttered with drift and litter, its wooden dock inundated, tilted green and sagging, waterlogged and sinking slowly with the weight of liverworts.

I explore farther, reaching into the inlet until I start to feel lost. Rowing back, I locate the new public ramp, a dusty parking lot and the floating dock where boys fish amid plastic soda bottles. They give me directions to a convenience store, "Up the road," to the anticipated treasure chest full of ice cream bars.

It's hard not to be disappointed with my dreams of Point Pleasant.

Here, at the confluence with the Ohio, the Big Kanawha River drains a major watershed from West Virginia. Along with barges and towboats, river traffic and commerce, I notice how things swept down from the past of one become the future of the other.

A SERIOUS BUSINESS

Eating is a serious business, yet hunger forgives a lot.
Repetition and simplicity is the key—quickly fixed, no fuss meals
varied by spices: Portuguese, Mexican, Chinese or American
satisfies the palate and the stomach, all from a Primus stove
with a one-pan menu: paella, chili or stew, oatmeal and coffee.

Potable water is the premium, so bring extra for long stretches.
Never use creek or river for kitchen or bath, and remember
the heft and momentum of a well-provisioned boat
comforts like your body designed for weather.

With every anchorage and each day, my identity expands.
New friends on the *Morgan Truce* wave goodbye as Pelican skims
down Pond Run through a tournament of bass fishermen
casting into shadows of dock, snag and stump. Swiiishhh....
Ker-plunk! Swiiishhh.... Ker-plunk!

I set the oars and sweep, gliding over the flat black water.
With a joyful ringing, we fairly fly towards Greenup Locks.

The pool is quick. Water rushes through the willows, combing
saplings into wet colors of bark and leaf, of soft shelled
mud turtles clamoring off a tangle of Kentucky debris:
slick, ornamental, and vicious.

Approaching a two-mile 90-degree turn, I row only for steerage
and cross to the right—the spray chills, the water cold with rain.

Rising up, the river begins to have a difficult time bending
around the bend. It piles up, folds back, gets in its own way,
the turbulence hiding a long sandbar, surprisingly submerged
on the outside of the turn. Waves start to tumble beneath
their own surface, deflecting back into the channel.

Energies bunch up for a mile, and as I round the sharp bend the sandbar shears off, water back-flipping into escalator waves undercut from below. I'm caught surging, surfing down slopes, Pelican's bow rising from the troughs up into the blue sky.

Then, the lethal half-mile ends, and finally the river broadens, becomes bigger, wider, the sun hotter, the water soft and flat.

Under white cumulus the shoreline whispers, "Sleep. Sleep," but I don't.

FORTUNATE CREEK

The dragon leans through the oxbow,
curves through a steep valley of rock, past variations
of table, bench and shelf, beneath hammocks and crest lines,
along the sloped sky etched into sharp, dorsal ridgebacks.

Hills play high in the maples, the oak and pine,
changing shadows from sky to rock, tracing silhouettes
from vertical to plateau, to an isolated house with children
laughing on its red porch as I move far below, a small speck
in the breeze of early morning reflections.

Gray goats flit over gray rocks, chased by a shepherd
in a boat whose engine smokes along a trotline, fish buoys
checked, hauled-in, and baited, the valley widening,
a sandy floodplain for picnics, colored tents and ski boats.

It feels good to sweat and row,
making miles in a rhythm of oars, frisking like a wherry
through hay country and cornfields absorbing the heat,
weaving the switchbacks, breathing the river.

There is little else but distance and the space for thought.

Creeks do not tempt my imaginings. Sand banks appear
and disappear into the brush and bush as I row past terminals
abandoned by the river, the river calling me on and on.

By dusk, it seems I'll have to anchor out with the towboats.
I've been caught in the late evening without a place to go:
undercut banks are ten feet high, small creeks merely sloughs.
So I cross towards Yellow Bank Creek, farther down.

Dusty foliage and dried leaves sweep the river into a swath
where I suspect the entranceway to the creek lies—
a slight flow beneath the hem of a tapestry.

Half pulling, half-parting, I edge through shards of leaves,
dragging the dory through brittle twigs and spiky limbs.
In twilight, without a choice I expect a dreary anchorage
dingy and dark with bugs and snakes, until I break into the light
like a sigh, into a tremendously thoughtful openness.

Duckweed and maple surround the transparent pond
where the anchor slips down its white rope.
Minnows in the shallows erupt like miniature squalls
rippling and rattling across the surface, sunfish and crappie
in hot pursuit, while a gar hunts slowly around a snag,
poking its snout out.

Beyond the leafy curtain, a towboat thumps and clanks
and moves upriver past the sunset. Its pressure wave
undulates and surges beneath the dory, scattering Sirius
clouds into thin flakes as orange as coals in the blue sky
lingering into purple, the sun disappearing into ink.

If I could name this place, I would name it Fortunate Creek,
as it has calmed my anxious heart.

THE ESTUARIAL BRAIN

I awake to a rooster, and to insects
pelting the canvas which I fold back,
poking my head out into a blizzard of mayflies
tic-ticking as they mass above and around,
nicking one another with their wings, the air
filled with percussions of flight from shore to shore.
Up and back, along the creek and into the maples,
the water is covered with their casings.

Last night the larvae, the subimagos emerged.
This morning the males are swarming, the females
darting in to be mated by the primordial chemistry,
by the eternal clasping of desire.

Intricate unities become a bloom of life
after a year in the silt eating algae. Burrowing nymphs
have tired of holding the world together. They've burst out,
rejuvenated into flight, matured, rehearsed, and molting
into the night, replenishing the spirit of this place.

Mayflies in amber gossamer—the strength
of 300 million years—lift from the creek, guided
by the moon and sun, in dusty swaths clattering
their emergence, an Eros of silt from mud love.

Netted wings swarm each to each, the beauty bound
in tender fossil beats as one node of the creek's rich garden,
an estuarial brain of the insect intellect.

I stay and drift as they disperse—a few final mayflies
fluttering into the dry maples rattling on the noon breeze.

With sweat, my straw hat regains its yesterday's shape.
Hot and dry, the farmland ushers me downriver into sounds
of fireworks at Millstone Creek. The 4th of July campground
mushrooms with bright nylon tents and people moving
in dusk and dream, shouting and running with sparklers,
lighting the roar of roman candles, zinging the blasts
from rocket poppers.

I pass through drifting smoke speckled with pinwheels
and sky bursts to a secluded wooded bank out of range.
Celebrations dissolve into a vision of sparks and pops,
frogs joining in with their chorus of mud, rib-bitting
into the inky dark up and down the bank, evenly spaced
singing their madrigal: Rib-Bit. Rib-Bit. Rib-Bit. Rib-Bit.

Every five or six feet a new voice rises up
into a green, moist dot on the imagined shore. Rib-Bit.
Rib-Bit. Crunch-Crunch. A raccoon chimes in
with its musical pause. The universe keeps spinning,
the frogs go 'round and 'round.

OF BAYOUS AND PINE SAND

How like a river can a river be
When a river even changes in thought?

Listen to it whisperin', whisperin'
Listen to it whisperin' wide.
Listen to the river rattlin'
When the towboats go rattlin' by.

This river from my top most window
Wakens to the changin' season, too.
The winter-wild river white and icy
Beneath the stone slow blue.

How like a river can a river be
When the river even changes me?

I pass the first swamp, and the coal, utilities and aggregate
companies, and a terminal jutting out solely for molasses.

"Hey, Jakes! Yah. How ya' doin?! Good, good. Yah, this is Annie
up at Neville Island. Yah. Say, hey Jakes, listen. Could you send
a 3 x 5 tow of molasses? Yah. The folks here in Pittsburgh
want to make some gingerbread. Yah, that's right. Throwing
a big shindig. In about a week? OK. Wonderful. No. No,
we'll get that from the Great Lakes. Comes down the Allegheny.
They're already stampedin' the cows. Right. You too, Jakes!"

Southern heat greets us at Owensboro in the guise
of a wooden dock dried to a pulp, so evaporated that even
the red paint stands up on end, all the nails are drawn out
by the claw hammer of the sun. Only an artist's rendering
holds it in place. Tetanus shots are given free with dockage.

It also has no shower and no restroom. Not because of the heat,
or perhaps because of the heat. But I'm glad to be here anyhow,
safe and secure, tied up to a marina where I can sleep tonight
as catfish fishermen fish, drifting on multicolored city lights.

All night, towboats keep the dock awash with wakes.
Sleepy eyed, I clear the marina on placid water sparking
into combustible bronze.

Slowly, I adapt as changes work through my anxieties,
layer my personality, laminate my body like a truss—
new knowledge creeps over the bridge with its tonnage,
heat absorbs into my skin, sinking down to my melted bones.

I skirt the left bank of a pebble-studded earth
listening for a rhythm of river, noting the music between
slow leaves. There is hardly any current.

I get caught along a string of moored barges, two and three
deep, midway and close in, by a fast moving tow. At first I surf
the wake, but then it angles straight toward the barges. A gap
in the outer line, like a missing tooth, allows me through,
but the wakes ahead rebound back after having sloshed
into the sides of deeper barges. Merging into a jolt, I drag
my oars to brake the ride, surging through the gap,
cornered, surfing the wake, so I pull hard to starboard
and pirouette out again, stopping just short of old rusty barge
376, after an expert cue shot by the passing towboat captain.

"He sure was in a hurry. Probably, delivering that molasses."

I boll weevil out 'a there, away from all those rusty dents,
and take a salt pill, drink some water, the current weakening
into summer. I've lost lots of weight, and it's difficult to row
for an entire day. By 9 a.m., we're into the heat of afternoon.

So I stay honest and plan each day's run, as a ritual.
The repetition of effort keeps me focused on the going:
to stay with the river, to enter the rhythms and to struggle
with whatever the water has in mind.

Occasionally, I'm rewarded with what I call, "An emergence."
From the depths, a thought or experience is released, seeking
its image at the surface, rising from its chamber into sunlight,
myself growing lighter with the serenity that lingers
into a breezy kind of joy.

Mysteriously, the discipline of rowing prepares me
and by the doing, becomes a kind of answer as I row and row.

I land at French Island Marina for lunch under a tree,
but Pelican nips at her tether and leaps along the dock
like a squirrel. From a distance the marina was shaded, framed
in memory and hung on my wall of sky, but I've skipped
out of time, unaccustomed to the heat flitting through my mind
as miles, names, and people, worries and weather drift away.

Outlines merge and dissolve. Even towns, locks and dams
disappear as I pass, while time stretches into a vague horizon,
weaves its frayed tapestry from morning to noon to night
as I plan the day's run, celebrate each threshold with treats
or a float break, selecting the best anchorage I can predict.

Engaged with this southern river, I try not to battle it,
but rather to forge a gratitude for its reality, as harsh as it is
and as persistent, in spite of my protective imaginings.

There are no sights or sounds of birds any more
in Audubon country, just an immense concrete wall
of Alcoa Aluminum and Southern Gas & Electric as it rises
into a near cathedral under a continuous heft of heat.

THE RIVER AS TEACHER

In the grog of late afternoon,
fatigued and cradled in the shade by an arc of high mud,
I watch an ultra-light airplane with yellow pontoons
tilt and waver around the bend, coming upriver
in bright dragonfly colors, the propeller pop-popping
with its chesty drone, the goggled pilot one long
silky scarf of red and gold.

To the right, halfway down Diamond Island
I drop the anchor, pay out line and tie up near a stump.
I fix dinner, adjust closer-in as outboards idle to the far shore
plugging for bass. Under branches in the shoal water
speckled with snags, I drift into sleep.

Sunrise pools over the distant hills and treetops,
spreading out as if from some deep wound, the great sun
rising from the ground, a circular coal shimmering waves
of orangey red, like a soft fruit. It stops and hovers beyond
the silhouette of an elegant knife, a smokestack splitting
fiery doors, quivering with the first sight of earthly mist.

Immersed in the quickened color of damaged light,
my gaze bows inevitably down into the immediacy of boat
and oars, of feet and legs moving in misty morning energies,
heat rising into a scenic warning as if from some wild voice.

My hands hold pain in crescent finger bones. Scavenging
like crabs, they melt into flesh around the darkened oars,
a lengthening wake strengthening past pain as I pull away,
a seepy-eyed sunrise running red, fast in daggered light,
the source of all my red silence.

Today, the sunrise has fractured into shards, my spirit
into a brittle tree bursting with birds—a place I was not
meant to be. Rowing out of the red murk, my visions warp
and disperse, like an illusion the night lasts only so long.
I'm freed into earthly motions, into the blue sparks
of a damselfly resting on the gunnels, changing its perspective
occasionally to an oar.

I'm being shown how to move without moving.
It darns my spirit to the gentler tasks.
Then, it darts off,
skimming over the surface in a little puff of wind.

With its tutorage, I cross the metallic pond
of silence and distance and approach Mount Vernon,
a river town rimmed with fleeted barges. Miles stretch
before and around, shrinking Pelican onto bronze emptiness.

Beaver signs are in the willows and a red channel buoy
hangs from a tree. A five-foot gar spooks into splashes.
We pass sandbars birthing more islands, wetlands
that shelter ducks in the animated reeds.

After earth building, the river is cleaner and clearer.
Mosquitoes hum from the foliage, tumble out as a cloud,
a dark swarm for a woven tapestry. Carp rise like little moons,
and gar nose around the anchored boat.

Closing the canvas over the dory, I find a lantern,
then splotch the inside of my cocoon maroon with blood.

AN ORAL HISTORY OF THE MAMMOTH IN NORTH AMERICA

*—as told to Thomas Jefferson by a chief orator
of the Delaware Nation, circa 1779*

i.

He stood as if in celebration, a Delaware warrior in regalia:
buckskin leggings and breechclout panels, colorful shirt
and tapered scarf, deer skin moccasins and a bear skin turban
all intricately beaded with strong designs of white and purple
geometrics and floral patterns. Over his shoulder, across his chest
a wide band was attached to a paneled pouch worn at the hip,
ornamented with black turkey beard and two red dyed deer tail.

A fan of golden eagle tail was used to gesture toward the floor
and then into the heights of the room as if striking the war post,
as he began his oration, bold and melodious:

"Ten thousand moons ago, when naught but gloomy forests
covered this land of the sleeping Sun, long before the pale man
with thunder and fire at his command rushed on the wings of wind
to ruin this garden of nature—when naught but the untamed wanderers
of the woods, and men as unrestrained as they, were lords of the soil
—a race of animals were in being, huge as the frowning Precipice,
cruel as the bloody Panther, swift as the descending Eagle,
and as terrible as the Angel of Night.

"The Pines crashed beneath their feet; and the Lake shrunk
when they slacked their thirst; the forceful Javelin in vain
was hurled and the barbed arrow fell harmless at their side.
Forests were laid waste at a meal, the groans of expiring Animals
were everywhere heard; and whole Villages, inhabited by men,
were destroyed in a moment—the cry of universal distress
extending even to the region of that Place in the West.

"But the Good Spirit interposed to save the unhappy.
Forked lightning gleamed and loudest Thunder rocked the Globe.
Bolts of Heaven were hurled upon the cruel destroyers alone,
and the mountains echoed with their bellowing death.

"All were killed except one male, the fiercest of the race,
and him even the artillery of the skies assailed in vain,
as he ascended the bluest summit which shades the source
of the Monongahela, and roaring aloud, he bid defiance
to every vengeance."[1]

ii.

We retired to our host's library,
French wine warming us in the candlelight flickering
like feathers of the scissortail. All of us as happy
as the gentle, unbroken ancients.

Governor Jefferson, our kind host, then brought out
giant femurs and the large molars of an elephant
thought to inhabit still the far regions of the north.

Time seemed lost in that moment, as I remember,
gathered in the shadowy realm of imaginings.

Such was my evening with the Ordinary People, the Lenape,
our struggling friends and allies, we the rebels in Virginia.

---

[1]Thomas Jefferson, *Notes on the State of Virginia*, Stockdale edition, 1787 (Chapel Hill: University of North Carolina Press, 1982), 43-44.

100 MILES OF HEAT

The earth cares for us if we let it,
but riddles seem our usual response:

A river without water; Food we cannot eat;
Water we cannot drink; A swim we cannot take.

Having left the earth's nurturing
we construct mechanisms to bridge our disconnection:

Systems replace reciprocity; Distance saddens the journey;
An early morning sun remains unmercifully clear;
Our visions are sharpened to cutting.

I row and row.

Coal companies have Uniontown working. Several tows wait,
others idle downriver off Poker Point. We are stacked up
in line for Uniontown Locks. One tow, full of coal, is longer
than an island, and stretches upriver, taking five minutes
to pass in the deep trough of its elephant feet.

I row through farmlands, over the shallow basin
of Wabash River gliding down with its load of silt
where pirates once lingered in caves nearby to prey
upon the weak and unwary, the tired and naive.

Then, in one single inhalation of heat
the Ohio expands into slow water rippling over bars,
islands birthing from hidden channels that flow darkly
over fallen trees as regal as any Shiva. The downstream
pools are cauldrons bubbling with fish, with reflections
joining earth to sky.

Even in this vast space of place the heat lifts
into a vacuum, the distant throb of diesel engines
churning and bending out of sight.

Arriving at a pier splintered into gray wood,
Shawneetown is a terminal for coal barges, blistered trailers
and a silent mutt guarding an empty bar. All the people
have gone somewhere else.

On the burnt grass of a deserted park, I find a vertical pipe
with a spigot that works. Hot water at first, then warm,
then cool gallons over my head, my face and neck,
over my shoulders and arms, down my spine, my legs
and feet into a broadening puddle of dirt and brown grass.

Stalking the twilight, blue herons circle the boat,
or remain motionless on the curving limbs of snag.
Tungsten feathers merge wing with shadow, eyes bright
yellow with black rings, toes as thick as fingers.

Inside the boat, the canvas fills with hieroglyphics,
with abstract paintings in blotches, splotches and smears
in an array of red from dead mosquitoes, all different
at each anchorage. Some are aggressive, some not;
some sting, while others you'd hardly notice.

The house specie is most common,
then the smaller tree-hole, then the diminutive
summer mosquito, cute but thirsty.

I sit facing aft in my canvas cocoon
folded back for any slight breeze.

In the early morning, Pelican whispers away
as I've learned to keep oiling the leathers and oarlocks.
By noon the shoreline lengthens into limestone cliffs,
a levee of fractured blocks built by giants into ledges, nests,
and little caves where I feel espied by eagles, ambushed
by pirates hidden in the twisted cedars poised on the crest.

At Cave-in-the-Rock, I carouse for cool drinks
and good information. After provisioning I walk up
through the surrounding forest. It is a real snake day.

They rustle in the dried leaves near the rocks—garter snakes
all charged up, vibrating their joys beneath bead eyes,
flashing down burrows to disappear into coolness
under the knotted roots of maple and pine.

On top of the hill, dwarf cedars shade the restaurant.
The river lazes below, glazed by the kiln of sun.

When I return to Pelican, I find her high and dry, poised
like a huge marshmallow on a chocolate colored sandbar.

Using the oar, swirling the shade
of cottonwood like a spoon, I pass the old Fish Market,
its catwalk twisted and tilted, the shanty sagging,
the shadows edging over the curl of its swayed roof.

I ease past Sarah Lusk's ferry landing,
then past a fishing camp stagnant with cobwebs, beer cans
and Styrofoam cups. Then, to Plew Island where I anchor
for the night, well off in deep water, heading upstream.

I sit at the opened canvas and fan myself
with my big straw hat. I sit, fanning and listening
with just the right flip of the wrist.

In the morning, swamps and bayous stretch left and right,
the river narrowing between rocky ledges, the water strong,
shouldering into curves, shearing the cliffs, carrying us
past inactive quarries, canyons of silent stone,

machinery that echoes in the hewn valley, like the radiant,
unfinished landscape of some ancient, abandoned city.

Hand tools, buckets, blue shirts and lunch pails
exist as a form of light, as translucent workers walking home.
A barge grounded on the amiable shore rusts into scrap.
Glazed by Kentucky heat, these stones, this kiln of place
whispers with the whoosh of oars gliding past.

I'd like to take a swim, but not in this shimmering sluice,
not in this mirage, metallic and as caustic as a chemical drum.

The horizon bends and disappears at the shoreline.
The river serrates at the bleeding of the world,
reflects into a thin and malleable uncertainty
lifting into a blue, unhindered sky.

Hammered by the heat, I retreat into a motel room
at Golconda Marina, air-conditioned where the chrome shines.
A pink countertop, scattered everywhere with little soaps,
has pastel shampoos, and enough towels to shower all day.
I drift back and forth with visits to town, the roadside
crackling underfoot like ash.

Melding into the crowd I glimpse a face, gather a glance,
recover myself on the street, storing up bits of dialogue,
the town a hiatus from which I must depart.

Heat comes down onto the anvil. People have died in the cities.

ADDITIONAL ACKNOWLEDGMENTS

My thanks for the support of family, friends, and the following organizations. Without them, this work would not have been completed.

To Walt and Virginia Spurgeon in the building of the rowing dory, "Pelican;" the Greater Pittsburgh Aquatics Club for hosting the launch from Neville Island, PA; Mary Steller for a place to write during the winter months; Margaret Dimoplon, Robert Pyle, and Sue Brownfield for their encouragement; Master Kim and the students of the Mudokwon, Muncie, IN; Joe's Marina, Big Bone Lick, KY; the Matthew Hansen Endowment for Wilderness Studies, University of Montana; the Antiquarian Society, Worcester, MA; the UCROSS Foundation, Clearmont, WY; and Mike McKillip for putting into song the lyrics "How Like A River."

My special thanks to Sandie for her insights, suggestions, and unceasing belief in the manuscript, "OYO," from which these poems were selected. And to all those kind folks I've met along the way.

ABOUT THE AUTHOR

Mark B. Hamilton's previous poetry titles include the award winning chapbook *Earth Songs* and a volume of lyric poems, *Confronting the Basilisk*. This new chapbook collects a sampling from his journey down the Ohio River, tracing the Lewis and Clark Expedition route, a 3-year, 7,600-mile saga traveling on their approximate timetable and as they did by paddle and pack mule. The complete Ohio River manuscript, "OYO," was a semi-finalist for the Washington Prize, 2015.

His poems have won state and national awards, being published by journals in the US, UK, Greece, Japan, and Austria. He has edited two environmental publications: *Words On Wilderness*, University of Montana, and *Groundwork: a natural incentive*, Ball State University, and is proud to have founded and directed Native America Day, in honor of the First Nations People, Missouri Western State University.

Mr. Hamilton did his undergraduate and MA work at San Diego State University, and earned the MFA at the Writers Workshop, University of Montana. He taught English for twenty years as an Instructor, Professor, Graduate Faculty Member, and Contract Faculty Member. He now lives on Florida's Gulf Coast in a traditional bungalow with his wife, Sandie, and their two cats, dividing his time between poetry and fishing.

His website is www.MarkBHamilton.WordPress.com.
His email address is markhamilton98643@yahoo.com.

www.ingramcontent.com/pod-product-compliance
Lightning Source LLC
LaVergne TN
LVHW041505070426
835507LV00012B/1349